SURVIVE IN THE MOUNTAINS

BY CHRIS BOWMAN

BELLWETHER MEDIA · MINNEAPOLIS, MN

™

Are you ready to take it to the extreme? Torque books thrust you into the action-packed world of sports, vehicles, mystery, and adventure. These books may include dirt, smoke, fire, and chilling tales. **WARNING** : read at your own risk.

This edition first published in 2017 by Bellwether Media, Inc.

Library of Congress Cataloging-in-Publication Data

Names: Bowman, Chris, 1990- author.
Title: Survive in the Mountains / by Chris Bowman.
Description: Minneapolis, MN : Bellwether Media, Inc., 2017. | Series:
   Torque: Survival Zone | Includes bibliographical references and index.
Identifiers: LCCN 2016000478 | ISBN 9781626174467 (hardcover : alk.
paper)
Subjects: LCSH: Wilderness survival–Juvenile literature.
Classification: LCC GV200.5 .B679 2017 | DDC 613.6/9–dc23
LC record available at http://lccn.loc.gov/2016000478

Printed in the United States of America, North Mankato, MN.

TABLE OF CONTENTS

Plane Crash! ———————— 4

On the Mountain ———————— 8

Finding Shelter ———————— 16

Eating and Drinking ———— 18

Making Fire and Signals — 20

Glossary ———————— 22

To Learn More ———————— 23

Index ———————— 24

PLANE CRASH!

Autumn Veatch and her grandparents are flying a small airplane from Montana to Washington on July 11, 2015. At first, the flight goes smoothly. Then they hit a rough patch of air.

The plane gets lost in a cloud, then drops below it. It crashes into the side of a mountain! Autumn crawls from the **wreckage**, but her grandparents do not survive.

"It was white, then I saw trees, then we crashed."
-Autumn Veatch

"It started feeling a little bit hopeless 'cause I had no idea where I was at all."
-Autumn Veatch

Autumn is burned and injured from the crash. Still, the 16-year-old follows a river downstream for two days. She drinks some water, but she is afraid of getting sick.

Autumn spends two nights near the river.
Finally, she finds a trail. She follows it to a
parking lot. Two hikers give her food and
drinks. Autumn is safe!

ON THE MOUNTAIN

Many activities bring people to the mountains. Sports like rock climbing, skiing, snowboarding, and hiking can be a fun way to spend the day.

But mountains also hold many dangers. **Altitude sickness** can lead to dizziness, headaches, and exhaustion. This makes falls and other accidents more likely. Some cases can cause serious illness.

GET USED TO IT

Before hiking high in the mountains, give your body time to adjust to the thin air. Climb slowly to lower the risk of altitude sickness. Descend if you still feel sick.

MOUNTAIN GEAR CHECKLIST

 high-energy food

 matches

 extra clothing

 cell phone

 ropes

 tarp

 whistle

 first aid kit

 sunscreen

 sunglasses

 water bottle

 hat

Weather in the mountains can change quickly. Thunderstorms, **flash floods**, and blizzards can form in minutes.

Thunderstorms often strike mountains on summer afternoons. **Descend** below the **tree line** and seek shelter if a storm approaches. Avoid open areas, especially near water, metal, and lone trees.

KNOW THE SIGNS

Changing wind direction and strength are signs a storm is coming. Other signs are low, dark clouds, a drop in temperature, and increased humidity.

In cold areas, avoid **frostbite** by covering all skin. Keep clothing clean and dry. This will also protect against **hypothermia**.

Be careful to avoid areas where **avalanches** occur. These snow slides happen most often on steep slopes. They are more likely after a fresh snowfall. Broken trees can show where avalanches have fallen. Travel above these areas.

DRESSING FOR THE MOUNTAINS

thick hat

light
under layer

thicker
middle layers

weather-proof
outer layer

gloves
or mittens

wool socks

hiking
boots

COLD CLIMB

For about every 1,000 feet (305 meters) climbed, the temperature drops about 3.5 degrees Fahrenheit (2 degrees Celsius).

Be aware of which animals may be near you in the mountains. Most do not want to attack, but will if surprised. Make a lot of noise to warn bigger animals to stay away.

Small animals can also be dangerous. Always shake out clothes before putting them on to check for spiders, scorpions, or other bugs.

COMMON GROUND

Mountains cover about 25 percent of the Earth's land surface.

WHEN ANIMALS ATTACK!

BLACK BEAR
fight back; try to hit it on the nose with a stick or rock

GRIZZLY BEAR
avoid eye contact and play dead; spread legs to make it hard to roll over

RATTLESNAKE
place hands and feet carefully while climbing; back away slowly if you hear a rattle

MOUNTAIN LION
try to appear bigger and yell loudly at it; make as much noise as possible

FINDING SHELTER

Shelter is your first concern if staying overnight in the mountains. Shelters below tree line offer the most protection. Above the tree line, big or piled rocks protect from storms. Use a blanket, **tarp**, or other material as a roof.

In snowy areas, a **trench** or cave can offer shelter. To make a cave, dig a tunnel in deep snow. Poke a small hole in the ceiling for **ventilation**. Then cover the entrance to trap in heat.

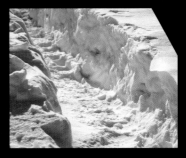

STAY WARM

If trees are nearby, use branches and sticks to build the shelter. A bed of leaves and pine needles can help keep you warm.

EATING AND DRINKING

Be sure to drink enough water in the mountains. You breathe more in thin air. This makes your body lose water more quickly.

If your water bottle is empty, boil water for one minute to make sure it is safe to drink. Always melt clean snow and ice before consuming it. Eating snow lowers your body temperature.

MOUNTAIN FOOD AND PREPARATION

Always know what plants and animals are found in your area.
Only eat foods you know for certain are safe.

Food: dandelions
Eat: raw

Food: soft pinecones
Eat: boiled or roasted

Food: inner birch bark
Eat: raw

Food: pine needles
Drink: boiled, for tea

Food: bugs
Eat: roasted

Food: oak acorns
Eat: raw or roasted

MAKING FIRE AND SIGNALS

A fire warms you during a night in the mountains. However, snow and wind make it hard to maintain. Build the fire behind rocks or in a low area to protect it.

Smoke from the fire can be a signal for help. Reflecting sunlight with a mirror also signals to airplanes. Use branches to write messages to rescuers in the sky. Stay calm until you are rescued!

MAKING A BOW DRILL

A bow drill can start a fire if you do not have matches or a lighter.

MATERIALS: two flat pieces of dry wood, a sturdy stick, a bendy stick (bow), string, tinder

1. Carve a circle into each flat board to fit the ends of the stick
2. Attach string to each end of the bow
3. Loop the string around the stick
4. Hold the larger flat piece on the ground with your foot
5. Fit the stick into the circle, and keep it upright with the other flat wood piece
6. Spin the stick by moving the bow back and forth until it starts smoking
7. Place tinder near the smoke to help the fire catch

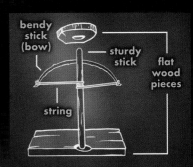

bendy stick (bow)

sturdy stick

flat wood pieces

string

WALK IT OUT

Stomping calls for help into the snow can also signal rescuers. Shadows make the message clear across long distances.

GLOSSARY

altitude sickness—illness caused by less oxygen in the air in high places

avalanches—masses of snow, ice, and rocks falling quickly down a mountainside

descend—to go down

flash floods—floods that happen in a short period of time, usually caused by heavy rainfall

frostbite—a condition in which skin and tissue are damaged because of cold temperatures

hypothermia—a condition in which the body loses heat faster than it can produce it; hypothermia causes body systems to shut down.

tarp—a large piece of waterproof material used to cover things and keep them dry

tree line—the height on a mountain above which trees do not grow

trench—a long hole dug into the snow

ventilation—a way to allow fresh air into a closed space

wreckage—the remains of something that has been damaged or destroyed

AT THE LIBRARY

Goldish, Meish. *Lost on a Mountain.* New York, N.Y.: Bearport Publishing, 2015.

Shone, Rob. *Defying Death in the Mountains.* New York, N.Y.: Rosen Central, 2010.

Yomtov, Nel. *Edmund Hillary Reaches the Top of Everest.* Minneapolis, Minn.: Bellwether Media, 2016.

ON THE WEB

Learning more about surviving in the mountains is as easy as 1, 2, 3.

1. Go to www.factsurfer.com.

2. Enter "survive in the mountains" into the search box.

3. Click the "Surf" button and you will see a list of related web sites.

With factsurfer.com, finding more information is just a click away.

INDEX

airplane, 4, 20

altitude sickness, 8, 9

animals, 14, 15, 19

avalanches, 12

bow drill, 21

clothing, 12, 13, 14

dangers, 6, 8, 10, 11, 12, 14, 15

fire, 20, 21

food, 7, 19

frostbite, 12

gear, 9, 13

hypothermia, 12

quotes, 5, 6

rescue, 20, 21

safety, 9, 11, 12, 14, 15, 18

shelter, 11, 16, 17

signal, 20, 21

snow, 12, 17, 18, 20, 21

temperature, 11, 13

tree line, 11, 16

Veatch, Autumn, 4, 5, 6, 7

water, 6, 11, 18

weather, 10, 11, 16

wind, 11, 20

wreckage, 4